Disclaimer: The book does not guarantee success as a Franchisee, provide details or infer the procedure of investing, or other alternative asset investments, or other associated tax and/or legal information. If you decide to choose that investment path, we recommend that you consult with an accredited Owner Managed IRA advisor, CPA and/or legal counsel for your specific situation. This book does not promise, imply or in anyway state any level or degree of investment success.

ISBN 978-0-557-77346-6

9 780557 773466

OWNER MANAGED IRA FUNDS
HOW TO BUY A FRANCHISE WITH YOUR RETIREMENT FUNDS

BY

DANIEL CORDOBA

CO-AUTHORED BY LYNNE SHELTON
& JASON POWER

IN COLLABORATION WITH SONIA ST. JAMES

AES Educational Sales Products

http://www.IRATraining.com

TABLE OF CONTENTS

SECTION 1: ABOUT OWNER MANAGED IRA PLANS

This book is intended for the individual investor who wants to manage their retirement investing using their individual retirement account (IRA or 401k). It also provides a method to determine the Owner Managed IRA investment plan that fits their needs.

Our goal is to teach you how to purchase a Franchise with your retirement funds. Use this book to become knowledgeable and enable yourself to select and purchase your Franchise while building your retirement funds.

Important Points

Throughout this book there is the mantra of the following benefits you will enjoy with your Owner Managed retirement account – these important points are:

Absolute investment decision authority – you have Owner Managed control over your investments without custodial intervention, review fees or delays.

Checkbook control – you have the ability to write your own checks without custodial fees.

No asset value fee - you pay a fixed, small annual custodial fee regardless of your success.

Litigation protection – The LLC structure makes litigation against the retirement account very difficult.

For more information, guidance and assistance contact Asset Exchange Strategies toll free at 866.683.5228.

There are many other strategies and methods of growing your investments and you can purchase additional educational materials on Owner Managed Retirement investments at IRATraining.com.

Why They Became So Popular

Owner Managed retirement plans are sometimes referred to as self-directed plans. Since 1974 a person could place real estate, notes or other non-traditional assets in their retirement. Of course, at that time almost anyone could make a decent return in the market and the perceived need for a portfolio with non-traditional assets was minimized or discouraged by traditional brokers and other professionals.

All that changed after the dot.com bomb, CEO scandals and September eleven. Real estate investors were making very good profits and the stock market was floundering. People who owned real estate or had friends in real estate were looking for options to bolster badly beaten retirement accounts.

That trend has not diminished since we first introduced our clients to Owner Managed IRA's in 2000. After placing a multitude of Owner Managed plans, our experience is that the demand is becoming stronger.

Difference Between Traditional & Owner Managed Plan

Traditional Wall Street retirement funds are generally limited to stock market investments; hence you have little control over the fluctuations of the stock market and the factors that influence it such as mergers and acquisitions, interest rates, wars, political instability, Fed Chairman's statements or policies, and Presidential campaigns. Owner Managed retirement plans allow you to make the decision what you'll invest in, and they provide you the ability to manage your chosen assets.

New Terms to Learn

If you're investigating Owner Managed IRAs you'll need to learn the terminology. An Owner Managed IRA investment plan is an IRA program in which you as the investor direct the investment in or out of the stock market. The most popular investment is real estate. These accounts are generally administered and controlled through Owner Managed IRA custodians.

However, as you will learn in the following text you can be in complete control. The Owner Managed retirement plan provides the IRA holder with many advantages: Checkbook control, Litigation protection of assets beyond state protection limitations, Ability to invest without obtaining permission, Flat custodial fees regardless of amount invested.

Who Are The Players?

Custodians

In the early 2000's when Owner Managed IRAs became popular, custodians were the focal point. Their role, however, is very limited. They cannot give advice - that would constitute conflict of interest. His limitations therefore became your limitations. However, every IRA must have a custodian. Our Owner Managed retirement plan provides compliance to all the requirements yet providing you with lowest overall cost structure and control, and there are times when control means the difference between loss and gain.

Facilitators

Retirement facilitators are firms that provide a similar product to our Owner Managed retirement plan but do not offer advice or ongoing support.

- o Limited or No investment strategies or products. No advice offered or vested interest or obligation to you or your investment

- o No implementation once you are on board

- o Primarily offer checkbook control, BUT no other benefits

- o Expensive, almost $500 to $1,000 more than Asset Exchange Strategies Advisors.

You can visit **IRATraining.com**; the largest education offering of Owner Managed retirement investment materials, and download self-study materials.

Attorney Groups

Traditionally expensive, complicated instruments, no investment advice, and no investment strategy offered. Most attorneys are (and should be) too busy creating instruments and therefore unable to play market detective for promising investment opportunities.

- o Cost prohibitive. Your final bill could be in the tens of thousands
- o Offer legal advice and the ability to gain checkbook control. It ends there
- o Limited or no investment strategies
- o No implementation
- o It's the first one they have ever tackled; are you sure you want to risk that lack of experience?
- o Success story of Starting Small & becoming very successful

In today's news we are barraged with news about the "Mortgage Meltdown" perhaps this is the perfect time for you to take advantage of a market segment that has created tremendous opportunity.

Example Investor

The following is an excerpt from Maria Fee, CEO of one of our partner companies, Remi Knox. Remi Knox specializes in notes and today in the Mortgage Meltdown they are doing a great business safely placing private money in safe private loans. This is a great example of an investment for a person who does not have the interest, time or experience to invest directly into real estate.

"As an investor I have spent a lot of time and money self-educating to understand real estate. I wanted to understand how to better control my investments instead of handing over my hard-earned savings to financial advisors who are still working to make a living. I believe in diversification like so many advisors chant.

A few years ago I was just about to buy an eight unit apartment complex. I ran my numbers, calculated my anticipated expenses and profits, made plans and knew what yield I should make from my 80-unit nest egg. What I did not plan for was a shooting that occurred on the property two weeks before I was scheduled to close on the property. That same night, 34 families moved out. Had I owned the property, I would have lost much of my anticipated yield for many, many months to come.

Regardless of my power planning, I would have little control of my financial returns in the first two years of my investment. I was back to feeling I had little or no control over my investments: I wanted safety, low risk, control, and known returns on my money. I kept studying, asking questions, seeking mentors, and finally found a well-hidden area of real estate – the notes business!

I discovered I could own the financing on a real estate transaction versus dealing with blue-collar issues such as:

o Unexpected repairs, expenses, and vacancies

o Increasing taxes

o Employee theft

o Contractor delays and cost overages, tenant

o Lawsuits

o Trash, toilets, and termites

I learned that I could use my brains not my brawn to invest in real estate. I could have collateralized investments, name my interest rate return, insure against property loss (my collateral), never received a phone call in the middle of the night, and still be diversified and invest in real estate!

Owner financing creates real estate notes. It is not a sexy investment topic but it is probably one of the most amazing financial investments we can own. This creative financing technique works in good and bad markets; rural areas and cities; and residential, land, and commercial properties. Owning the financing on the property rather than the property itself allows you to control the property without the risks, hassles, negotiations, and costs of ownership!

No banker or financial planner will tell you owner financing is a great investment. They don't get commissioned on real estate notes! Their sole purpose is to collect your money, invest it with the hopes of increasing your investment, and regardless of their success, earn commissions."

It should be noted that Maria Fee successfully grew this business from just a start up to one that was sold for a handsome profit. I personally know Maria and I believe that she would agree that most investors if they were to apply themselves could achieve the same success she achieved.

How To Know if You Are an Owner Managed Investor?

Investors have a maturation process. Just as with any other process there are certain steps and in this case there are four basic stages to an investor's development.

Advisor managed portfolios – The most basic and common form of investment is the advisor-managed portfolio. The investor for many different reasons such as time constraints or limited knowledge may not want to learn the basic skills needed to manage a portfolio. This first stage investor is reliant upon advisors and generally allows the advisor to make all the investment decisions.

Second stage, Owner Managed – This investor has taken responsibility for his portfolio and may have a basic understanding of risk management and market segments. In the world of securities investment this investor is generally with Fidelity or Charles Schwab

The successful investor at this stage has learned about macro and micro portfolio diversification. For example, an investor at this point has learned that advisor portfolio management can be very expensive. He may have learned about market segmentation and if another decline in the market should occur he knows that not all segments rise and fall at the same time.

Third stage, Owner Managed – This investor is now engaged in nontraditional markets. This requires learning how to conduct due diligence properly, the investor is now often the financier of ventures whether they are his own or other ventures. However, as with the first stage the investor still requires the need for a custodial representative and Owner Managed custodians offer the investor procedural support.

This procedural support can be very expensive and may hinder the ability to make the best deal. An example may be an investor that has moved his Owner Managed IRA away from the Owner Managed brokerage and has funds invested with an Owner Managed IRA custodian. In this case the investor has both traditional and non-traditional assets but still requires the assistance of an Owner Managed custodian.

In this stage, the custodian allows by permission, for the investor to purchase an asset, the custodian holds title to the asset, the custodian charges an asset fee based on the value of the portfolio and manages the assets transactions and charges of fee for each transaction.

The biggest difference between this custodian and the traditional custodian is the allowance of non-traditional assets such as directly owning real estate. This investor is almost there but has one more stage to evolve into and that is the fourth and final stage.

Fourth stage, genuinely Owner Managed – This investor has stepped into the last and most rewarding stage. The investor now has complete control of his assets and is keeping all of the earnings by self-managing his assets. The investor's IRA operates a Venture™ IRA LLC and has provided the investor with the most complete control of his destiny with the greatest return on investment.

The Owner Managed investor enjoys the following benefits:

- Absolute Checkbook Control of your IRA assets: You can write checks from your IRA with custodial-free ease.

- Investment Decision Control of Your IRA funds: You are the CEO of your financial portfolio. Get approval for your investment through a requirement-free process!

- Asset Protection through the Venture^{TM} IRA LLC: Your retirement is safeguarded from Creditors and Litigators with Comprehensive Asset Protection.

- Most Minimal Custodial Costs Offered: A once a year minimal custodial fee will keep your wallet full and will insure you are not spending your retirement years counting pennies, but counting memories.

- The Most Overall Value across the Board: You get all of the above, plus investment strategies and products that are all included.   Through a network of non-traditional asset professionals.

Is an Owner Managed investment plan right for you?

Yes! If …

- You want checkbook control of your IRA;

- You want to make your own investment decisions without the need of a custodian;

- You want asset protection for your retirement beyond what is currently available;

- You want the lowest possible custodial fees;

- Find a Trusted IRA Advisor If you're considering a Owner Managed IRA, you need to think about:

- Finding an Advisor you are 100% comfortable with.

- If you're considering a Owner Managed IRA, you need to think about:

The Owner Managed Plan Advisor

Your Owner Managed IRA investment Advisor should only deal with the IRS code and what it explicitly says. No policy interpretation, no asset fees and no requirement to report back on the desired asset purchase.

Protect Yourself From Prohibited Transactions

An investor has the same opportunity to commit a prohibited transaction with a custodian as they would if they were on their own. Why? Because each and every custodial website states they do not and cannot offer advice. If the custodian offers advice they become liable and they'll send you back to "your" advisor for help.

If you are like most people investigating Owner Managed IRAs you have learned that there are very few "advisors" who understand the IRA rules. We will only provide to you what the IRS says you can't do and under what circumstances. If desired, a compliance review and confirmation of correct structure will be provided.

You Make The Investment Decision

With custodian involvement the investment decision is theirs not yours as to what can be bought. Now the possibility of missed investment opportunity is present.

More FAQ'S on Owner Managed Investing at

MyRealEstateIRA.com/faq

SECTION 2: GOAL SETTING & STARTUP ACTIVITIES

Now that you have determined the type of Owner Managed IRA plan that fits your needs, your next step is to define what you want to accomplish with your investment plan.

The first step to starting your endeavor is to define what you want to accomplish with your Owner Managed investing plan. You will succeed and thrive much faster if you can articulate your goals, and how they will be accomplished accompanied with an action plan.

Having a clearly defined goal, and being able to articulate it will enrich the outcome when you meet with your Advisor.

If you are a serious investor, we highly recommend you write a business plan and include a well thought out financial forecast. The goal setting exercise is not meant to replace a business plan – it is merely a reference point as you get your business organized and running.

Here is a guide to state your goals and objectives on how you will achieve them.

Goal Setting

Goal: State the primary outcome you want to accomplish with your owner managed plan.

    Example: Achieve 10-12% ROI annually

State Your Revenue Objectives: Be specific and realistic.

Year 1 $ _____	Year 2 $ _____	Year 3 $ _____

Objectives: Write 3 key objectives that must be met in order for you to achieve your goal.

Examples:

1. Set up and fund your owner managed 401k) plan
2. Purchase Franchise
3. Implement Franchise marketing / sales plans

Startup Activities

You'll also want to review the short list of business startup activities we've provided.

Remember, as in any new business your success will depend on your ability to negotiate, stick with it attitude and activities, organization skills, and the quality of people you decide to work with.

Here is a guide to the first steps you'll want to take.

Basic Activities List (Not listed in sequence or priority)

Set-up your office – including computer and software, printer, fax machine, broadband service, furniture, and other office equipment

Set-up a tracking and filing system for business transactions

Write your business plan

Organize the documents and forms you'll be using for easy access

Set-up payment schedule for self-employment taxes (If applicable)

Decide on name of your business

Print business cards

Create budget

Develop your marketing plan

Re-review the transaction documentation you'll be using

Schedule training and other essential time identified

Identify the service professionals you'll be working with and build relationships with each

Your Additions:

SECTION 3: INVESTING IN A FRANCHISE

Buying a Franchise

The decision to buy a franchise is often a hedge against the uncertainty of starting a business from scratch. Much of the work that goes into designing the atmosphere, targeting your desired demographics, and marketing to the target is done for you. If you choose a good franchise, your brand identity will already be well known and people will know at a glance what business you are in and will (hopefully) have a positive reaction.

In return for all of the work a Franchisor puts in to making a franchise successful, they typically charge a franchise fee (which varies with the franchise) and a percentage of the profits.

Franchise Financing With Your 401(k) Plan

An Owner Managed 401(k) is plan setup for your company. As manager of the company, you can act as the Trustee for the plan's monies. This enables you to self-direct investments on behalf of your 401(k).

Most traditional IRAs and 401(k)'s are limited to investing in traditional investments such as mutual funds. However there are many other viable investment choices and options, such as buying a Franchise, that are not available through these traditional means.

How It Works

An Owner Managed 401(k) is a 401(k) plan setup for your company. As manager of the company you can act as the Trustee for the plan's monies. This enables you to self-direct investments on behalf of your 401(k). Purchasing a Business with an Owner Managed 401(k) allows for a debt free start-up since no bank loan is required, and no bank loan means no interest payments.

This enables faster wealth building. Also, any revenue your business generates can go back into building your business rather than paying off debt. The absence of debt means a much faster and smoother journey to your ultimate destination.

The 401(k) Owner Managed plan allows you to use your own retirement funds to purchase their Franchise.

This is accomplished in six steps:

1. Create Entity (generally a C-Corp)

2. Create and setup the 401(k) Plan for the company

3. Rollover your IRA or 401(k) monies to new 401(k) Plan

4. Setup Checking Accounts

5. 401(k) Plan Invests in the new Entity

6. Purchase the Franchise

The process of setting up the 401(k) plan:

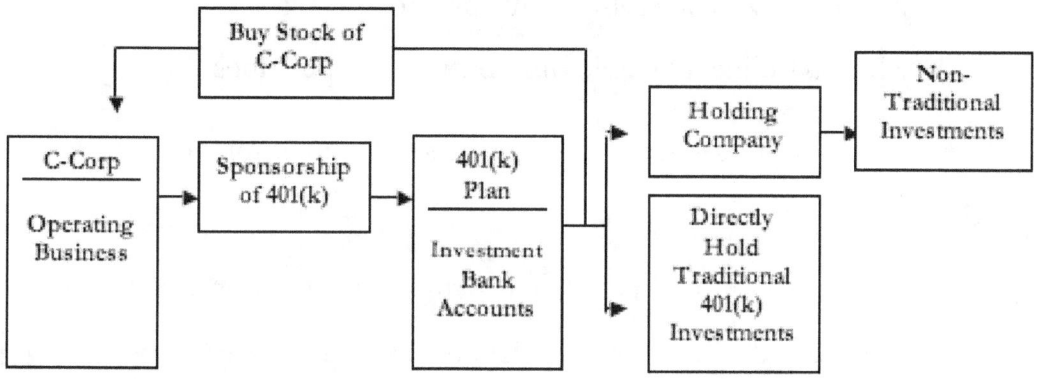

How You Benefit

- Investing in Yourself - Using retirement funds to start your business is an investment in yourself.

- Realizing More Control – Unlike risking your retirement funds in the stock market, you are in charge of your own future by managing your own investment (your franchise)

- Debt Free Start-up – Why incur debt with a bank loan when you could put your retirement funds to work for you.

- Low Overhead – Not having to take out a bank loan means no interest payments or debt to start your franchise. The initial revenue your franchise earns can then go back into the business instead of paying off debt. This allows you to build your business faster.

- Tax Savings – Asset Exchange Strategies 401(k) program allows you to utilize your retirement fund to finance your business, while avoiding a taxable distribution and penalties.

- Contributions - Make 401(k) employee and employer contributions

The landscape of a franchise is a win-win situation. Simply put, the Franchisor provides the business structure and in return receives a franchise fee. The 401(k) Owner Managed plan is a smart alternative to the traditional bank loan, uses your own retirement funds to help you realize the opportunity of owning a franchise.

Purchasing a Franchise with a Self=Directed 401(k) allows for a debt free start-up since no bank loan is required, and no bank loan means no interest payments.

This enables faster wealth building. Also, any revenue your business generates can go back into building your business rather than paying off debt. The absence of debt means a much faster and smoother journey to your ultimate destination of success.

There has been much talk about The ROBS Memo and as we'll discuss there are plenty of critics. However, it must placed into perspective for example, the memo clearly starts out that "Although we do not believe that the form of all of these transactions may be challenged as non-compliant per se, issues such as those described within this memorandum should be developed on a case-by-case basis."

That is IRS speak for some people are abusing these, and there are not clear guidelines established so we'll look at compliance as they go along. As the memo is read the treasury department is pointing out what the auditors should look for and how they are to be measured.

So even though there may not be the clarity some would like to see the memo clearly describes the objective, standards and process by which these plans are measured.

Comments On ROBS Memo

By Jason Power, ESQ. Shelton & Power, LLC

Note: Promoter (or promoters) is often used as a negative adjective by those who view the ROBS memo as a 'declaration of doom'. Because there are several facilitators or advisors, which legitimately follow the law, we will use the term Advisor in place of promoter.

What Are ROBS & Why Are They Turning The Franchise World Upside down

In late 2008 the Department of the Treasury determined that a new type of retirement plan was coming into existence and was circumventing the tax system with great results.[1]

These retirement plans, called **Rollovers as Business Startups, or "ROBS"** as coined by the Department of the Treasury have been creating a stir in the retirement planning and tax industry that is causing both retirement advisors and tax professionals to reexamine their positions and product offerings. After much examination and analysis of these new retirement plans, the Department of the Treasury, ("DOT") drafted a memorandum on October 1, 2008 explaining the history, drawbacks and procedural questions that arise from these ROBS.

Operating essentially as tax shelters, ROBS are marketed by retirement professionals, or promoters, as a method of using retirement funds to start up new businesses or franchises with zero tax implications.

---

[1] http://www.irs.gov/pub/irs-tege/rollover_guidelines.pdf

Primarily, ROBS are used to deal in employer stock. This type of transaction is intended to avoid applicable taxes which are typically associated with standard tax-deferred accumulation accounts which the DOT believes creates a multitude of potential tax problems which will be discussed later in this chapter.

ROBS were first discovered and examined by the Employee Plans Examinations department of the DOT. After being created by the retirement professional industry to assist budding entrepreneurs purchase businesses and franchises, the Employee Plans Examinations department received requests for determination letters as to the plans' legal compliance. Although the plans received favorable determination letters, the DOT and the Internal

Revenue Service took notice of these transactions and how they skillfully navigated the normally applicable taxes and penalties assessed against early retirement withdrawals. Although the plans change from promoter to promoter, throughout the many variations of the plans, some elements and the overall purpose have remained the same.

With many people out of work due to layoffs in recent years, some are turning to their retirement accounts for survival much earlier than anticipated. Several people in this demographic profile are also using their retirement accounts to start businesses of their own to become economically self-sufficient through use of their retirement, to replenish their savings, and to salvage something to leave for their children.

ROBS are increasingly becoming the preferred mechanism to perform this.

ROBS serve various purposes, but according to the DOT, they are being primarily used by entrepreneurs to fund the establishment of businesses or franchises, as touted by multiple websites. [1] According to the DOT, ROBS "are designed to allow a newly created business entity to retrieve available tax-exempt accumulation funds from its principal in exchange for its capital stock, simultaneously avoiding all otherwise imposable income and excise taxes that would ordinarily apply to the transaction." [1]

ROBS are created in a variety of different ways by various promoters; however the overall framework remains unchanged. ROBS "are designed to allow a newly created business entity to retrieve available tax-exempt accumulation funds from its principal in exchange for its capital stock" [1]

To enable a ROBS customer to utilize their retirement funds tax-free, promoters create what are called plan documents for the client, which involve the creation of a corporation and a 401(k) plan. In a typical transaction, the promoter works with the owner of the account, a.k.a plan participant to create a C-Corporation to sponsor the retirement plan. Afterwards, the C-Corporation adopts a standard 401(k) type plan.

Employees, if any other than the owner, are permitted to roll funds into the new 401(k) from their personal retirement accounts and in return are issued stock in the new company.

This rollover allows the plan participant and any others involved to roll their retirement funds into the new company without incurring any taxes or early withdrawal penalties, thus allowing the funds to be used to purchase a franchise or business. Most promoters charge a fee of approximately $5,000 and with some promoters a $1,000 annual fee for keeping up with the plan documents.

With the IRS looking into more and more ROBS transactions and audits looming in the future for many of these plans, it is advisable to work with an experienced ROBS promoter and a CPA to make sure that you are compliant with all applicable laws on an annual basis.

There are many skeptics of ROBS transactions. But as with anything that is misunderstood, those that do not understand react with skepticism and criticism. With this being said, both the IRS and most writers who look into ROBS transactions have more negative things to say than positive. Several of the negatives look at how the plans are operated by the plan owners, not necessarily how the plans were created.

Therefore, before you look into some of the benefits and drawbacks of ROBS transactions, it is wise to make sure that you understand where many of the criticisms are drawn from.

The first critic of ROBS was the DOT who found ROBS questionable because "they may serve solely to enable one individual's exchange of tax-deferred assets for currently available funds, by using a qualified plan and its investment in employer stock as a medium."[1] This worries the DOT because this method of operation may help to avoid the pre-distribution taxes and 10% withdrawal penalty under the Internal Revenue Code Section 72(t) that are typically assessed on these types of transactions in other retirement options. In other words, they are not happy with the tax loophole being found and used.

Most issues primarily arise during an audit of the ROBS, which is becoming more common, or when the person drafting the ROBS requests a determination letter from the DOT. Initially, the DOT issued favorable letters for ROBS in almost all cases as the primary makeup of the plan was to take a standard prototype plan and make a minor amendment allowing investments into employer securities.

Since that time, the Employee Plans Examinations department has become more stringent on their review of these determination letter requests.

After receiving multiple requests for determination letters, the DOT has been forced to create a "Specific Examination Project" to review the plans. The "Specific Examination Project," after looking into many of these plans have found significant disqualifying operational defects including, but not limited to: "employees in some arrangements having not been notified of the existence of the plan; do not enter the plan or receive contributions or allocable shares of employer stock; failure to value plan assets; failure to file plans; or a creation of a business for the plan that has failed to survive."[1]

Many critics and analysts of ROBS have cited that there are two potential legal problem areas:

1. Violations of non-discrimination requirements, and

2. Prohibited transactions

For those who disfavor ROBS because they possibly violate the non-discrimination requirements, the rationale is that because only one person is involved, the principal, he or she is the only employee who benefits from the transaction.

The fact that other employees are not permitted to have stock in the employer is what causes some people, including the DOT, to believe that some transactions violate anti-discrimination laws within the Internal Revenue Code.

The theory behind this criticism is that an employee stock option program through the company's 401(k) must be offered to all employees, not singled out for one individual. The IRS in these cases has determined that on a case-by-case basis, these transactions may violate the anti-discrimination laws.

However, most ROBS transactions solve this problem by creating the C-Corporation with the plan participant as the sole officer/ employee of the corporation, which prevents any other employees being in the company, therefore making the discrimination issue a moot point.

Other opponents and skeptics of ROBS argue that the transactions lend themselves to the possibility of entering into prohibited transactions, which in many cases takes the form of self-dealing. First of all, we need to discuss what a prohibited transaction is.

This is where most concerns arise among both plan participants and retirement advisors. According to the Internal Revenue Service, a prohibited transaction is a "transaction between the plan and a disqualified person" which is prohibited by law.[2]

Now that we have that settled, we all understand completely, right? But, who qualifies as a "disqualified person?" The IRS gives an exhaustive definition of a disqualified person; however, the primary type of disqualified person who causes the most trouble is a "member of the family" of a plan fiduciary, a person providing services to the plan, an employer for the plan, or a direct owner of 50% or more interest in the plan.[3]

This type of prohibited transaction comes into play when the plan owner chooses to purchase a vehicle, house, office, etc. for a close relative or in many cases, purchases a time share or vacation type home for rental, but chooses to inhabit the rental themselves.

---

[2] http://www.irs.gov/pub/irs-pdf/p560.pdf
[3] http://www.irs.gov/pub/irs-pdf/p560.pdf

All of these examples qualify as prohibited transactions under the disqualified person section of the Internal Revenue Code. Because these "prohibited transactions" exist, it is imperative that you work with a well-versed ROBS Advisor.

With an annual maintenance program, you can call to obtain support about the status of a proposed transaction before you actually cross the line into the "prohibited transaction" realm.

ROBS can be a favorable method of financing for starting a new business or franchise. Just remember to always be aware of the penalties for failing to comply with the applicable laws. No one wants to fall prey to penalties, some of which can be as high as 110% or more of the transaction for non-compliance.

As with any drawback, there are also benefits. By many advocates of ROBS transactions, the 2008 IRS Memorandum setting forth the concerns over ROBS, has been the best selling point for ROBS. The IRS has set out many of the potential procedural problems that promoters have encountered, enabling them to be remedied and touted as further benefits and services billed for.

The problems listed by the IRS have given promoters the information necessary to pass along to their clients as a warning of what needs to be done by the plan participant if they want to prepare for or avoid a future audit.

In light of all the criticism of ROBS, it should be remembered that the overall concept is not illegal, but is fully permitted under the law. The only group that does not like ROBS is the government, and that is because they are losing taxable money on this tax loophole.

Any illegality of the transaction only occurs in the later years of the plan, when the documents are created incorrectly or when the plan participant does not follow proper protocol with the government regarding filing appropriate documents.

In 2010, with numerous people out of work and even more looking to start their own business, there is surprisingly little credit available to the average budding entrepreneur. These instances are where ROBS promoters and the transactions themselves can be of great benefit to both the budding entrepreneur and the economy as a whole.

Individuals looking to start their own business, who do not qualify for small business loans or simply cannot afford the monthly payments stacked with interest, can turn to ROBS.

Use of their retirement funds to help fund their future by reinvesting profits into the business allows them to establish the business instead of using the funds to pay off loans. The franchise industry has taken notice of this with some Franchisors even promoting the idea and pushing for certain companies to be used.

With the franchise industry in particular making up over a third of the US economy, many people turning to franchising are using their retirement funds to invest with. Any franchise show in America has at least one supplier promoting the use of ROBS transactions to purchase franchises, and an increasing number of franchisors are suggesting those companies and transactions to assist buyers.

As the DOT and the Internal Revenue Service look deeper into the ROBS issue, it will be best for those looking in the direction of ROBS to do their homework. With ROBS promoters being listed by the IRS, you should remember to always look deeper into the retirement advisor to make sure that their qualifications match what they are advertising and that their experience matches what the IRS has labeled them as.

Through some research into the IRS and maybe a phone call, the average person can find much of the information needed to properly evaluate a company.

It is wise to remember that although many retirement advisors allege approval of their ROBS transactions by the IRS, most are operating based solely on the adequacy of the forms used, not the overall approval of the plan makeup.

Another good option for making sure your ROBS transaction is legal, is to have a ROBS Audit performed. Many companies can perform an audit of your plan to make sure that both the obvious and non-obvious violations are caught and brought to your attention before it is too late.

However, because the IRS has determined that the specific facts of each ROBS transaction will have to be reviewed on a case-by-case basis to make sure they are in compliance with the established laws and guidance, it is best to have a qualified attorney, who has worked with ROBS promoters, review your plan documents for compliance with all relevant laws.

Overall, it is best to create a relationship with your Retirement Advisor and CPA. Several of the potential problems discussed above may be avoided entirely by working with your Retirement Advisor or CPA closely when creating and updating your plan. Remember the goal is to use your tax funds for you, without any of the tax penalties; that is the beauty of ROBS.

SECTION 4: DETERMINING WHICH FRANCHISE IS RIGHT FOR YOU

By Lynne Shelton, Esq. Shelton & Power, LLC

With over 66 franchise industries and hundreds of franchise opportunities, determining which franchise is right for you can be a daunting task. This chapter will first evaluate the best practices for eliminating the franchises that are not right for you. Then, within your whittled down list, we will dive further into how to pick the right franchise for you.

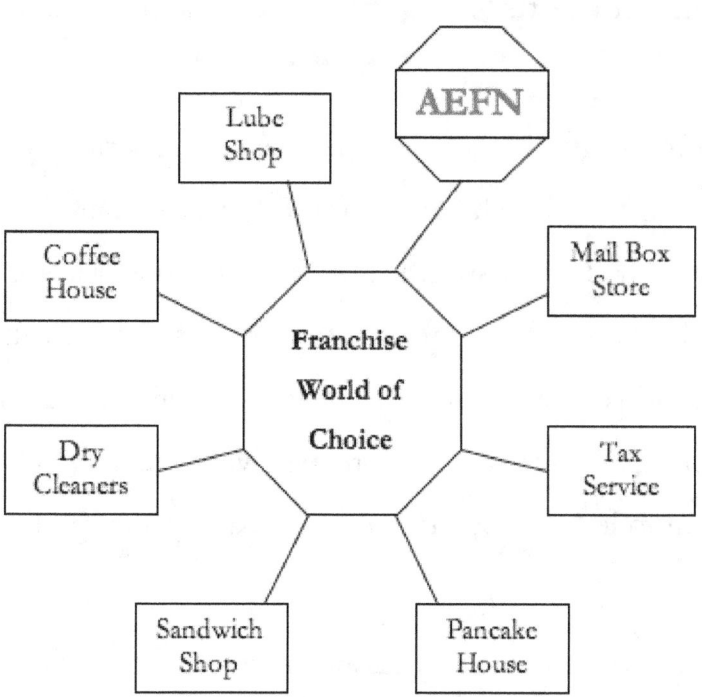

Eliminating The Franchises That Are Not Right For You

Buying a franchise is not necessarily an easy way to owning your own business. However, it usually is a lot easier than starting a business by yourself from scratch. Buying a franchise eliminates a majority of the bad business decisions that come from a person's lack of experience. Franchising also gives you an inside view into what a successful business looks like after it has become successful and profitable.

If you create a model by yourself, the only view you have is the one within your dream. As reported by Barclays Small Business Survey in 2007, "Over 65% of new businesses fail within the first five years; however, Natwest reports 93% of franchisees claim profitability."[4]

But how do you begin this process? Earlier you've written down your goals. Next ask yourself, why do I want to buy a franchise? What truly is important to you? Be very specific and write down all the answers you come up with. This will become a self-awareness checklist that should be used when looking at all of the industries available for franchising. One undoubted answer that most prospective franchisees write down is that they want to learn or obtain knowledge about that particular business.

Franchising allows you to start your business using the Franchisor's know-how and learned expertise throughout the years they have been in

_____

[4] www.whichfranchise.com. last visited May 5, 2010 copyrighted as of 2009.

business. Additionally, the franchisor should be there to help train you, promote you, and assist you as needed. Now think about those elements, and decide which ones are the most important to you. Is it the training? What about the advertising and promotion program? Are you a self-starter or do you know that you will definitely need additional assistance? These are main focus points to help you weed out franchise systems that are not in your best interests.

Let me explain, if you know you need additional assistance, or that you are "thickheaded" as my grandmother used to say, you will want to eliminate the industries that provide constant change and fast-paced environments that will allow you to avoid the feeling of frustration that will undoubtedly come your way in those environments. Another industry evaluator is the training provided by the Franchisor.

Almost all franchise systems require you or your manager to successfully complete the Franchisor's training program. If the franchise model deals with Sales and Use Tax and requires an accounting degree level of understanding, and you are horrible at math, that is a franchise industry to eliminate.

We recommend you complete the AEFN Franchisee Self-Assessment Exercise: it can be obtained at http://www.iratraining.com/Franchisee_Self_Guide.html

This self-assessment guide is designed for you to make an informed decision if being a franchise owner is right for you. Based on what you learn from the exercises in this document, you, and AEFN will be able to determine if owning an AEFN Franchise is mutually beneficial. In addition you will have a better understanding of:

- What makes a successful franchise business owner

- What skills do you need to master and make money in the business of selling Owner Managed IRA plans

- The realities of being a business owner and of doing the job

- How much money does it take to start up and operate your franchise, including the amount of cash do you need to cover your general living expenses in your first, second and third years in operation

In addition, the self-assessment addresses your skills, abilities, and readiness regarding:

- o Essential core competencies of a successful Franchisee
- o Job characteristics and your relationship to each
- o Setting goals and realistic business expectations
- o Financial preparedness
- o Complete understanding of your products
- o Marketing skills

- o   Sales skills
- o   Financial, accounting, and reporting
- o   Operations
- o   Customer relations

The self-assessment looks at your skill set, your experience, background, and personal characteristics.

Your responses to the various sections in the self-assessment will help you to eliminate industries, and to choose the franchise best suited to your aptitudes, experience, and abilities. Don't be afraid to cross off a whole industry if it requires a skill set that you do not feel comfortable with. If you do not feel comfortable speaking with people face-to-face, odds are you never will be. So do yourself a favor and eliminate those franchise systems that require it. If you do not, you are only setting yourself up for failure.

Now the fun task. Evaluate and write down your hobbies. What do you enjoy doing for fun? What is it that you always wish you had more time to do? Are you an avid scrap booker? If so, don't eliminate any industries that are craft-based. Do you love everything sports? If so, definitely don't eliminate retail sports stores, golfing outlets, sporting goods, or sporting clothes type franchise industries.

Now flip it. Write down the hobbies that you've heard about that you think are ridiculous. If you have no idea what the thrill is in scrap booking, eliminate its industry from your list. If you cringe every time you walk into a restaurant that has a football game on then a sports related franchise is not for you.

Next, take a look at your moral and ethical compass. Ask yourself, what matters to me, what upsets me, or what organizations do I belong to? Write all of these down as additional avenues for evaluation. If you are a member of PETA, you can most assuredly eliminate all taxidermy franchise systems.

Now take a walk on the dark side, what are your fears? Not your economic fears, your personal fears. Does the possibility of being robbed make you wake up with night sweats? According to the 2006 FBI Uniform Crime Reports 447,403 robberies were reported to the police at the rate of one per minute in the United States.[5] 8.3% of all robberies occurred in late-night retail establishments like gas stations or convenience stores where a gun was used to force the cashier to hand over money.[6] 80% of all franchise owners have reported working in every position possible within the franchise system, which means that you may be exposed to the possibility of robbery.[7] In fact many Franchisors require the owners to spend time and learn all of the duties in all of the employment positions.

---

[5] Mueller III, Robert S., Director, Federal Bureau of investigation, United States Department of Justice, Washington DC 20535, *Preliminary Semiannual Uniform Crime Report for 2006*. Available at: http://www.fbi.gov/ucr/prelim06/index.html
[6] Id.
[7] International Franchise Association. Available at: http:// www.franchise.org.

Since being robbed is a very real possibility in any retail situation, if this aspect makes you too afraid, you would do well by yourself to eliminate retail franchise industries that require being open after dark.

However if you are analytical and think you can overcome your fear here, there is some help in the same report. Approximately 44.5% of all robberies occur on the street, directly against the person, and are called a strong-arm robbery.[8] This is where someone robs another by using force or fear against him or her to steal something. Either way, it is wise to take your fears into serious consideration.

Franchising is work and work is supposed to be fun and being afraid is not fun when trying to run a business.

You should now have two lists; one that contains all of your "That Would Be Fun" industries and one entitled "Stay Away From" industries.

How To Pick The Right Franchise

Now that you've narrowed your choices down to a few select franchises, take another look at your moral and ethical compass.

Go back and take a look at the list you created earlier; and then use this chart to collect and organize data on the franchise(s) you're considering.

---

[8] Mueller III, Robert S., Director, Federal Bureau of investigation, United States Department of Justice, Washington DC 20535, *Preliminary Semiannual Uniform Crime Report for 2006*. Available at: http://www.fbi.gov/ucr/prelim06/index.html

Franchise Names ⟹			
Opportunity to meet my Goal			
Opportunity to meet my objectives (1, 2, and 3)	1	1	1
	2	2	2
	3	3	3

How long in business
How long in their industry
Franchise market position
Provide marketing-execution support
Provide cash flow management
support
Provide comprehensive training
Provide human resources support as
needed
Type of experience with franchising

Territory assignments

Provide territory growth and control

Certified franchise executives on board
or management team

Strong board or management team

Litigation - pending or finalized

Credit for advertising and marketing
fees when you sponsor a non-profit or
cause

Member of International Franchise
Association (IFA)

Member of VetFran

Member of MinorityFran

Industry requires working weekends,
Sunday, or holidays

Requires change in lifestyle

Compare the following using % or estimated dollars:

Build out costs (hard assets)

Ongoing working capital needs

How long -

How much -

Break even point

Rapid ROI

One of the best ways to learn about a system is to evaluate it through a various websites that do a great job of collecting franchise information around the world.

1. I recommend first looking into the International Franchise Association's website at http://www.franchise.org.

2. Secondly, you can review franchises through http://www.WhichFranchise.com, which also has the additional benefit of showcasing both the European and United States franchise systems. Both websites have a plethora of franchise systems broken down by category, price range, as well as capital expenditure requirements.

I encourage you to request information from many of the Franchisors that are within the industries on your "That Would Be Fun" industry checklist. However, do not torture yourself. If you can only leverage $150,000 for your entire franchise purchase and build out, do not look at any franchise system that requires over $300,000.

> Over-extending yourself financially is a primary downfall for many franchisees.

Typically around 50% of the entire capital expenditure can be leveraged through promissory notes, or leases. Once you have collected many of the franchise system's informational brochures, it's then time to evaluate them within a Franchisor -- Franchisee relationship basis.

From all of the brochures you have gathered, pick the top two or three franchise systems that you are most interested in that fit all the requirements you have outlined throughout this process. We will discuss specifically how to evaluate a franchise, so gather your franchised brochures and follow the evaluation and checklist procedures in this text.

Evaluating The Franchise You Select

Congratulations, you have selected a franchise (or several) that's a fit for you - or is it? We will take a look at specifically how to evaluate a single Franchise Disclosure Document, and from those findings you have the information you will need to make an informed business decision. You will determine whether or not to negotiate the franchise purchase and enter into a franchise agreement with that particular franchisor. The below information will help you to take an in-depth look into the elements that will drive your business relationship with the Franchisor.

It is important that you complete all of these steps so that you will thoroughly understand what will be required of you if you should choose to join that particular franchise system.

It is equally important for you to hire a franchise attorney to assist you in this review process. Do not rely on general attorney practitioners; business, real estate, or commercial attorneys as they do not have the in-depth knowledge into the franchise world that is required to help you make an informed decision. And at all costs avoid attorneys that specialize in litigation, they do not understand the word negotiation.

When a prospective franchisee retains Shelton & Power, we go through very thorough evaluation of the franchise system. Although I cannot explain the legal aspects within this limited space, we will go through the business aspects utilizing a sample form that we have designed for our clients, attached at the end of this chapter.

The Franchise Disclosure Document (FDD)

So where do we begin - at the beginning of course. I think it's only befitting to first describe what an FDD is.

The Franchise Disclosure Document (FDD) is a disclosure document given to prospective franchisees, i.e. you, by the Franchisor.

- The FDD discloses information on all areas of the franchise.

- The FDD also includes legal documents such as franchise agreements, area developer agreements, non-disclosure agreements, guarantees and other legal documents that the Franchisor will require all new franchisees to sign prior to being awarded a franchise. It allows the prospective Franchisee to research the franchise thoroughly and ultimately decide if it is the right franchise for them.[9]

- The FDD is vital as part of any prospective franchisees due diligence as it essentially covers everything they need to know about the franchise business to make an informed decision on whether the franchise is right for you.

- The beginning of the FDD contains a cover page that outlines the total estimated costs including the initial franchise fees as well as some of the risks for that particular franchise system. Note

---

[9] *What is a franchise?* Available at: http://whichfranchise.com/us/article.cfm?articleID=756. Last visited August 11, 2010.

however, that many of the risks are standard boilerplate language that is required by the federal government or state agencies.

- The FDD ensures that if you live in one of the 22 advanced requirement states that the Franchisor is currently registered within your state. Within the "state cover page," it should also list what states that franchise system's FDD is registered in. There are total of twenty-two states that require advanced registration and approval, or advanced exemption or notice filing before the Franchisor can sell in those states.

If for example you live in California, which is in a registration state, and you do not see a listing on the state cover page showing that the Franchisor is registered in California, you can contact the California agency that handles the state administration for franchise registration to request whether or not the franchise system is registered in the state.

You should find a list of the state administrators located either within Item 2, or as a separate Exhibit to the FDD. If you determine that the franchise is not registered with the state, you should report that franchise to the state agency, as well as the Federal Trade Commission through their website at www.ftc.gov, or you can let us know at mailto **info@SheltonPower.com** so that we can assist the company in becoming legally compliant.

Evaluating The Franchisor

The next area to evaluate is the Franchisor. Some of the items to jot down in your notes section would be things like:

- How long have they been in business

- How long have they been in this industry

- What type of experience do they have, what type of experience with franchising do they have, and

- How strong the board is

- You will also want to jot down any litigation that is listed within the FDD. Ensure that there is a full explanation as to who sued whom, and for what. The FDD should also contain the legal outcome and dollar amounts involved, if applicable. This will give you great insight into whether the Franchisor is litigious and constantly suing their franchisees for the smallest of details or if they are simply protecting their brand.

Also, look to see if the Franchisor or any of its members have any US-based or international bankruptcies. If they do, this is certainly one of the areas that you will want to discuss with the individual that filed for bankruptcy within the franchise system. It is my experience that no one is above needing a clean start at one point in life. Take the time to ask the reasoning behind what caused the filing of the bankruptcy; this will give you great insight into the Franchisors life as well as their morals.

Item 5: Lists the initial franchise fees for single units as well as multi-units. Make sure that you write down any discounts that may be available to you through multi-unit purchasing, Vetfran, or MinorityFran, if applicable.

Item 6: Lists all other fees that you are responsible for paying throughout you relationship with the Franchisor. These could include royalty fees, grand opening advertising, marketing fund contributions, local advertising requirements, software fees, phone systems, audit expenses, insurance requirements, training fees, additional training costs, optional operations assistance fees, legal fees, renewal fees, and manual fees. Be sure that you list each and every one of these fees so that you can do a thorough comparison between franchise systems.

Item 7: Although the total capital investment is listed on the cover page, Item 7 breaks down the individual costs for the items that make up the total capital investment. You should see listed within this table, at a minimum, the following items: initial franchise fee, travel and living expenses while at training, real estate for rent deposits, leasehold improvements, if applicable, the site inspection and review, utility and miscellaneous security deposits, furniture fixtures and equipment, opening inventory, insurance, additional funds for operating expenses for three months, and a miscellaneous column as a catch-all.

It is very common practice to see a low and high range for all of the categories listed within the table. It is also common practice to have different tables listing all of these items, where the numbers would vary greatly, based upon a possibility of a different type of location for the franchise system such as a mall location vs. a standalone restaurant.

Also be sure to read all of the notes to Item 7 that follow the tables contained within the FDD. This will give you great insight into how the Franchisor arrived at these figures and any particulars or assumptions that the dollar amounts are based upon.

Item 8 & 16: Deal with restrictions imposed against you on the sources of products and services you can purchase and sell.
Within this portion of the FDD there can be additional items besides services or products you offer to the public or to your customers. It is not uncommon to see discussions regarding the business's location or approved site, or what type of furniture and fixtures will be allowed. Occasionally, you can also find requirements regarding the computer, software and bookkeeping requirements, although these are typically located within Item 11.

It may also reflect certain benefits that the Franchisor currently receives from the vendors they require you to use. Make sure that the FDD discloses what percentage of the Franchisor's income is derived from vendor kickbacks or commissions. This section should also give you clear direction as to whether or not you have the ability to suggest a different supplier. This could become important if one of the Franchisor's approved vendors must ship a product a great distance to your location thereby charging you a much higher average cost of goods than other franchisees in the system. You want to make sure that you try to locate non-proprietary products from vendors that are within your geographical area.

Item 9: Known in the industry as the big roadmap. Here you are given a brief and concise overview of the main obligations within the franchise system and where they are located within the Franchise Agreement and FDD. If you are looking to purchase more than one franchise, this table should also direct you to the applicable obligations within the Area Development Agreement or Master Franchise Agreement, which ever your particular franchise system uses.

Item 10: Pay special attention to Item 10 that deals with financing options available from the Franchisor. If the Franchisor offers in-house financing or prearranged financing arrangements, Item 10 will list it.

Item 11: If Item 9 is your roadmap, Item 11 is your legend.

Typically Item 11 will be the largest Item within the FDD. By statute, it must lay out all of the Franchisor's assistance, advertising, computer systems and training obligations to you.

Based upon the federal laws, you will see this laid-out in seven sections:

1. The Franchisors pre-opening obligations, then;

2. A listing of typical length of time between the date the you sign your franchise agreement and when you will be able to begin operations;

3. Franchisor's assistance during the operation of the franchised business;

4. Advertising and promotion responsibilities;

5. The computer/software /phone system requirements:

6. Information regarding the Operations Manual along with the Table of Contents for their Manuals; and

7. Information regarding their obligation for training you, which must also include a breakdown of the number of days and type of training.

The Franchisor must break down whether or how much training will be done within the classroom or on-the-job training and where that training will take place, for example whether it will be at the Franchisors headquarters or at your local franchised business. This information is extremely important because it lays out the requirements that the Franchisor must provide for your franchised business.

It is advisable that your franchise attorney assists you with evaluating the level of assistance the Franchisor is guaranteeing that they will be providing. Unless you have been a franchisee before, you will need a Franchise Attorneys assistance to know whether the guaranteed amounts of training are within industry norms, or if you are to be left untrained and on your own.

Item 12: Within Item 12, you will find information notifying you of how the Franchisor designates territories or whether they offer protected territories. For most franchise businesses, I would highly recommend only purchasing one that will grant you a protected territory. A protected territory means that neither the Franchisor nor other franchisees will be allowed to operate a competing business within your geographical area. This is typically one of the areas ripe for negotiation. Also look to this section for proposed penalties for the Franchisor or other franchisees that invade your protected territory. If there are no penalties, the value of your protected territory diminishes greatly.

Item 13 & 14: Deal with intellectual property owned by the Franchisor. Make sure that at least one trademark is being granted for your use. If there are no trademarks, then legally it is not a franchise. Most Franchisors take protecting their intellectual property very seriously. In fact, you will normally see provisions within these Items very clearly defining how you must assist them in policing and protecting their Marks.

Item 15: If you are looking for an investment only, you need to pay particular attention to Item 15. This section that deals with whether you have an obligation to participate in the actual operation of the franchised business. Most Franchisors prefer owner/operator franchisees. In fact owner/operator franchisees in the retail industry show a 75% greater chance of success than non-owner operators.[10]

Item 17 deals with all of the "what ifs." Officially it is titled "Renewal, Termination, Transfer, and Dispute Resolution"; therefore that should give you insight into how important provisions laid out in this table will be to your franchise agreement.

There are 24 statutorily required disclosures within Item 17. In order to be in federal compliance, the Franchisor must list the applicable provision, its location within the franchise agreement, and a quick summary of that provision's terms when dealing with any of the four topics covered under this Item.

---

[10] IFA SmartBrief. http://r.smartbrief.com/resp/xHuMdumdzgcVAuuofDafawcNJToM.

Item 17: Pay particular attention to provisions (a) through (h) (although all 24 are extremely important). The first few provide you with a length of term for your Franchise Agreement and if you have the ability to renew, the number of years that the renewal term will be for. It will also spell out in detail what requirements you must meet in order to renew the Franchise Agreement. A common provision within subsection (c) is that you must sign a general release waiving all known and unknown litigation claims that you have against the Franchisor.

This is a very common statement placed in the majority of FDD documents. However, many of the registration states will modify or eliminate this requirement altogether. Subsections (e) through (h) deal directly with termination. There are two types of terminations within a franchise system:

1. Termination by the Franchisor based upon curable defaults, and

2. Terminations by the Franchisor in which defaults cannot be cured

Let's talk about the latter first. Termination by the Franchisor in which defaults cannot be cured is a listing of the items that, if they occur, give the Franchisor justification to terminate your franchise agreement and take away your territory immediately or upon notice. Some typical actions would include misrepresentation or omissions in the application for the franchise, and failure to satisfactorily complete the training program, misrepresenting or reporting and accurate royalty fees greater than 2% on more than one occasion, bankruptcy, utilizing the confidential information or the trademarks in an unauthorized manner or running a competing business without prior permission.

Depending upon the franchise system and the franchise attorney utilized to create the franchise system; this particular list can vary greatly. The first type of termination, as termination goes, is certainly the better type - termination by the Franchisor based upon curable defaults. These defaults will also be listed in great detail; however, they will also list the amount of time that you have to cure them or to correct them prior to being actually terminated. Typically, you will see items such as failure to comply with mandatory specifications, receiving a health agency warning, or failure to make a timely payment. To cure these defaults, you simply must comply with your franchise agreement for the default.

However, be careful as there is usually a provision somewhere in the franchise agreement that if you receive too many notices of default with the right to cure, the Franchisor may choose to terminate your franchise by simply sending a Notice of Default. So it is imperative that you attempt to comply at all times with your Franchise Agreements contractual obligations.

Item 18: Specifically lists out Public Figures. Next, you get to see whether there are any celebrities within the franchise system. For the purpose of Item 18, a public figure, per the Federal Trade Commission, means a person whose name or physical appearance is generally known to the public in the geographic area where the franchise will be located.[11] If anyone within the Franchisor's company is known as an industry educator, author or speaker or has specific expertise in the industry, or has received awards within the industry, they would also qualify as a public figure.

You can also see the extreme opposite, where the persons listed under public figures are nationally known athletes, spokespersons, actors and actresses were other known and commonly referred to "celebrities." If your public figure is a celebrity, you should also see listed within this item the amount that the Franchisor is paying for the Endorsement Agreement, if applicable. If you have such a person in the franchise system you are evaluating make sure that you are given the right to utilize the celebrity's likeness in all of your promotions, advertising, marketing efforts. If you are not granted these rights, it greatly reduces the amount of benefits that you will receive personally from this arrangement.

Item 19: Titled Financial Performance Representations is one of those hotly debated topics within the franchise world. Financial Performance Representations equate to sharing either historical or

---

[11] Grueneberg, Susan and Hurwitz, Ann, (2008). *The FTC Franchise Rule: Analysis and Commentary*. American Bar Association, Forum on Franchising.

forecasted financial data dealing with profit or loss, sales information, cost of goods information, personnel requirements, and many other topics that you can utilize to forecast your own profitability. The franchise federal rule allows but does not require this information to be placed into Item 19. The Federal Trade Commission has issued standard verbiage for franchise attorneys to utilize when setting up item 19. Specifically, it states:

"The FTC's Franchise Rule permits a franchisor to provide information about the actual or potential financial performance of its franchised and/or franchisor-owned outlets, if there is a reasonable basis for the information, and if the information is included in the disclosure document. Financial performance information that differs from that included in Item 19 may be given only if: (1) a franchisor provides the actual records of an existing outlet you are considering buying; or (2) a franchisor supplements the information provided in this Item 19, for example, by providing information about possible performance at a particular location or under particular circumstances."[12]

Most Franchisors that offer Financial Performance Representations complete this disclaimer by stating further "Except for the sales analysis provided below, we do not furnish, or authorize our salespersons to furnish, any oral or written information concerning the actual or potential sales, costs, income or profits of your _____Franchise."

---

[12] Id.

If you are a business guru, a statistician, or an accountant, this section should be quite exciting for you.

However, if you are a normal entrepreneur, this is certainly an area to discuss heavily with your franchise attorney or certified public accountant. As far as the format for this section, beyond the disclaimer there is no such thing as standardization. Every Franchisor can give as much or as little information as they choose to depict their system in the most accurate light.

Item 20: Entitled Outlets and Franchisee Information has exploded over the last two years. It now consists of at least five tables of information displaying everything from the number of outlets that the Franchisor had three years ago to the total number of outlets at the end of the last fiscal year. You also see information regarding company-owned outlets as well as outlets have been terminated or not renewed. However, there is a huge nugget of information awaiting you in the section, although it's not normally housed actually within this section, it normally is displayed as an exhibit to the FDD.

What is this nugget? A list of current franchisees along with their addresses and telephone numbers as well as a list of terminated or canceled franchisees along with their contact information.

> You must, absolutely must, call each and every terminated and canceled Franchisee that the Franchisor has listed on this exhibit.

However, with that being said, please go into those conversations knowing absolutely for sure that there are canceled franchisees that will not be happy with the Franchisor. They will each have a sob story, a reason why the Franchisor failed them, or a horror story of competition opening close to them. Very few failed franchisees are humble enough to admit defeat was based solely on their own errors.

However, the information that they share with you can assist you in determining if there are any modifications that you may need to your franchise agreement or any additional requests that you may have of the Franchisor.

One such instance comes to mind; when a prospective franchisee learned from a failed/canceled franchisee that because they had not been in the industry before purchasing the franchise they did not pick up very quickly the technical aspects of the franchise system required. They shared with the prospective franchisee that in hindsight if they had only requested more training or stayed longer at headquarters, they felt they could have turned out a better product and therefore made their business a success with repeat customers.

This nugget of great insight allowed the prospective franchisee, who also did not have a technical background, to negotiate additional training at headquarters prior to opening along with additional assistance at the grand opening to ensure that their first customers would be as satisfied as the Franchisors latest customer. I recommend that you utilize the information you glean from the terminated franchisees in much the same way.

Therefore, be very accurate with the list of the excuses, reasons, and hindsight shared with you and utilize them to affect reasonable negotiations with the Franchisor. If the past shows that most franchisees with your type of background need more training, negotiate for it in the beginning. Use this information to help you become more successful as a franchisee. Most Franchisors physically ache whenever they lose a franchisee, so they are going to want to help you. Remember that most franchise systems are really just a family of business owners sharing and succeeding together.

Items 22 & 23: The last two items of the FDD, Items 22 and 23, deal with the contracts that you will sign if you become a franchisee, as well as acknowledging receipt of the FDD package. On the last page of your FDD is typically where you will find Item 23 known as the receipt page. The receipt page gives you standard legal requirements for both federal as well as state specific laws that deal with a "cooling off period" where you will be given adequate time to sign the franchise agreement or to submit any money to the Franchisor.

If you are in a non-registration state, the Federal Trade Commission requirement is that the Franchisor must provide the disclosure document to you 14 calendar days before you sign a binding agreement with or make a payment to the Franchisor or an affiliate in connection with the proposed franchise sale. This time can be sooner based upon state specific laws.

Also the receipt should identify all of the exhibits to the FDD, who your franchise seller is, listed by their personal name and title, as well as, the date of issuance for the franchise disclosure document. If this information is accurate, you should sign your name and date the receipt with the date you actually received the FDD, not necessarily the date that you are signing the receipt page.

FDD Exhibit: One of the exhibits to the FDD will be the proposed Franchise Agreement. Make sure that you read the entire agreement carefully, utilizing your FDD evaluation form, to ensure that all material provisions concur with the same provisions within the FDD. If provisions are different between the FDD and the Franchise Agreement, that may be a violation of federal law. Certainly it must be a topic of discussion with the Franchisor.

Different franchise systems will require different requirements of the franchisee, however, some common topics to be discussed within the Franchise Agreement should be:

- Definitions, grant of exclusive franchise,
- Fees,
- Term of agreement and renewal provisions,
- Approved location, proprietary marks,
- Trade secrets and other confidential information,
- Training and assistance,
- Manuals,
- Advertising and promotional activities,
- Accounting,
- Records and reporting obligations,
- Standards of operation,
- Franchisor's additional operations assistance,
- Insurance,
- Default and termination,
- Rights and duties upon expiration or termination,
- Transferability of interest,
- Right of first refusal if applicable, relationship and indemnification, general conditions and provisions,
- Dispute resolution and acknowledgments.

You most certainly will have a provision requiring of you a duty of good faith and fair dealing which requires "honesty in fact and the observance of reasonable standards of fair dealing in the industry" along with a statement asking you to acknowledge that you understand that the Franchisor is relying on you to bring forward, in writing, any matters inconsistent with the information set forth in so that Franchisor can correct any misunderstandings.

This request is to assist the Franchisor in finding and becoming aware of any franchise seller that is misstating or promising aspects to prospective Franchisors that the franchise system simply does not offer.

> If you have received any promises or financial information that is not contained within the FDD, you should place that information in writing and request specifically that it become part of your Franchise Agreement so that you may rely on it legally.

Your research should however not stop at the FDD. Most franchisors will not provide financial projections or estimates of earnings from the franchise unless they have also provided you with the Item 19 Financial Performance Representations. Even so, your best guidance is still to speak to existing and former franchisees. Remember to ask clear and precise questions concerning their experience with the franchisor, the support, the business of the franchise and their financial performance as it relates to their own franchise outlet. This information will go a long way in assisting you when making a final decision to join the $1 trillion industry of franchising.

Now that you have finished your evaluation of the franchise, remember to give a copy of your worksheet to your franchise attorney; however, keep a copy handy for yourself so that you will be reminded of all of the areas that you wanted to negotiate or discuss with the Franchisor. This list will also assist your franchise attorney in learning about your goals, fears, and areas of the agreement that may need further explanation.

Once you have decided on a particular franchise, the next step is to negotiate the franchise purchase.

Sample FDD Evaluation Form

Franchisee Name: _____

Franchise System: _____

Date: _____

Discuss With	Title of Section	Notes regarding Section - Areas that May Need Negotiation or Discussion with Franchisee
☐	Franchisor	
☐	Industry	
☐	Experience	
☐	Litigation	
☐	BK	
☐	Fees	
☐	Other Fees	
☐	Initial Investment	
☐	Restrictions on Sources	
☐	Z's Obligations	
☐	Financing	
☐	For's Assistance	
☐	Territory	
☐	Trademarks	
☐	Patent / Copyrights	
☐	Participate	
☐	Restrictions on What	

1

Franchisee Name: _____

Franchise System: _____

Date: _____

☐	Renewal / Term	
☐	Public Figures	
☐	FPR	
☐	Outlets / Zees Info	
☐	Financials	

Franchise Agreement

☐	Grant	
☐	Franchise Fee	
☐	Developer Fee	
☐	Area Rep Fee	
☐	Royalty	
☐	Advertising $	
☐	Grand Opening $	
☐	Training	
☐	Transfer Fees	
☐	Renewal Fees	
☐	Website Fees	
☐	Accounting Fees	
☐	Staffing	

2

Franchisee Name: _____

Franchise System: _____

Date: _____

	Fees	
☐	Late Charges	
☐	Supplier Approval $	
☐	Liquidated Damages	
☐	Insurance $	
☐	Begin Business Time Frame	
☐	Termination w/o Cure	
☐		
☐		
☐		
☐		
☐		
☐		
☐		
☐		
☐		
☐		
☐		
☐		
☐		
☐		
☐		
☐		
☐		

3

SECTION 5: NEGOTIATING A FRANCHISE PURCHASE

By Jason Power, Esq. Shelton & Power, LLC

Negotiation is a natural part of everyday life for some people, but others may find the concept terrifying. However, to a certain extent, everyone negotiates at some point during their lives, most on a routine basis whether they know it or not. From buying a house or car, to working with a spouse or children to make a decision about where to eat on a Friday night, everyone negotiates.

So what should be so different about signing a 60 plus page franchise contract that will govern your professional life for the next 10-20 years and will control the fate of your entrepreneurial and financial future?

In the franchise world, negotiations are done on a daily basis. Franchisees negotiate with franchisors to prevent being defaulted; franchisors negotiate with vendors to get their franchisees better deals.

So why is it taboo for many people to negotiate their franchise purchase? The reason for this question has been answered over and over again by people in the franchise industry, mainly by big franchisors with loud voices. Most of the answers that are being heard are that franchisors are not willing to negotiate any franchise purchase, no ifs, ands, or buts. However, in most cases, this is simply not true.

Most franchisors do not want to negotiate franchise agreements for one simple reason, it gives away some of the control that they treasure. Note: The typical franchise agreement is written in the franchisors favor, not the prospective franchisees.

Many franchisors site that they will not negotiate the franchise agreement because it will create a lack of uniformity in the system. This can be a valid point depending on what is being negotiated. However, in most instances, this is an attempt to shut you up. Do not let the franchisor succeed. If the franchisor continues to refuse to negotiate on issues that are extremely important to you, then it might be time for you to look into another franchise or bring in your attorney to help with the negotiations.

A good franchise attorney can assist with negotiations, however, be wary of using attorneys that have no franchise experience. Although attorneys carry the stereotype of being good negotiators, the franchise negotiator is a special breed. Knowing the ins and outs of the franchise agreement and what can typically be negotiated and what cannot is a skill that only a franchise attorney has cultivated over many negotiations. However, searching for a good franchise attorney can be almost as daunting a task as searching for the right franchise system.

One of the best sources for researching franchise attorneys is the International Franchise Association. The International Franchise

Association, or IFA, is a global organization geared towards the advancement of the franchise industry. Most franchise attorneys are listed with the IFA and can be easily accessed through the IFA's website for review. One secret is to find a franchise attorney who has come from a business environment before going to law school. Better yet, find one that has experience in the Multi-Level Market, or has an entrepreneurial background. This type of franchise attorney can provide additional insight to your needs.

Why You Should Negotiate Your Franchise Agreement

Now that we have discussed why franchisors do not want you to negotiate the franchise purchase, or franchise agreement, let's discuss why you should negotiate this priceless contract for your entrepreneurial future.

When looking at a Franchise Disclosure Document as well as the Franchise Agreement, you are being thrown into a plethora of numbers, statistics, legal jargon and various other terms and conditions that you may or may not understand. A good franchisor will work with their attorney to make these documents as easy to read as possible. But as stated earlier, beware. The franchise agreement is typically written in the franchisor's favor, not yours.

You are investing a considerable amount of your time, energy, and money to operate this business, bottom line it's going to be your future, which is why you must negotiate! Don't you think you should get the best bang for your buck? Is it worth some of your time and maybe an extra investment to hire a franchise attorney to ensure that you are getting what you want and deserve out of the business? Have you ever heard the phrase "two heads are better than one?"

Some franchise buyers believe that just because they are working with a franchise consultant that they automatically are getting the best deal possible. This is simply not true.

Most franchise consultants are getting paid 15% to 40% of the franchise fee to find you for the franchisor. This figure is staggering when you look at franchise fees ranging from $35,000 up to $500,000. Therefore, it is in the franchise consultant's best interest to guide you towards a high dollar franchise. However, this comment is not in any way geared towards turning you away from franchise consultants.

Franchise consultants can be some of the most helpful and informational guides when it comes to traversing the franchise jungle. Nobody, save the franchisor themselves, will know more about the franchise system as a whole like a franchise consultant. But as stated earlier, be wary and research the franchise consultant prior to following them through the jungle.

As with any industry there are better franchise consultants than others. Listen closely to what you hear and weigh the findings with your franchise attorney.

Other franchise purchasers like to attend franchise trade shows under the false assumption that the franchisor themselves will be present and they will learn the intimate details of the system. This is again, simply may not be the case.

Some franchisors utilize franchise trade shows as strictly sales pitch arenas where sales employees are recruited by the system, or in some cases local franchisees, to deliver a smile and a colorful explanation of the franchise system in hopes of luring in a franchisee. Always look past the suits and ties, the colorful displays and glossy folders and ask the hard questions.

If a franchisor or its sales associates are truly interested in you as a franchisee, they will take the time to answer all of your questions. Those systems that give you a pitch and then ask you to sign up for more information without answering your questions may not be what you are looking for.

How should you negotiate a franchise purchase?

Now we go on to the nitty-gritty. This is a question that we, as attorneys, are asked at each franchise trade show we attend. Note that we are not in three-piece suits with flashy displays and fake smiles. The short and simple answer to this question is carefully and calculating. Now, that wasn't so hard. Moving on.

Here's the long answer. Both you and your franchise attorney can work towards negotiating a franchise purchase. However, in some cases, you might be just as effective as an attorney. However, if your personality is not negotiation centered, you will most likely fail; therefore, you may want to hire an attorney. When deciding how you will negotiate the franchise purchase, there are a few questions that you need to answer.

What do you have that will be appealing to the franchisor and cause them to want to negotiate with you? List your talents and talk with your franchise attorney about them, he or she may see more of them in you.

What does the franchisor not have that you can use as leverage to obtain a good deal? Most importantly, what are you prepared to give up in order to possibly get what you want from the franchisor? Any good negotiations in the franchise arena must start with these and similar questions. By providing your franchise attorney your high and low offers, preferably ranked in priority to your business, you stand a better chance of obtaining results.

You must determine what should be negotiated. Often people jump straight to money when negotiating a franchise purchase, and many are turned away because of it. Remember, money can be saved in other areas of a franchise purchase that can add up to significant amounts.

Negotiate Your Territory

One of the first areas in a franchise agreement that can be negotiated is the protected territory granted to you. Located in Item 12 of your Franchise Disclosure Document, and spelled out in detail in your franchise agreement, you may have an area that is described as your "protected territory."

Note that some franchises do not offer protected territories that allow their franchisees to intrude into each other's territories. If you have a protected territory, then it is wise to think about your long-term goals with the franchise.

- Are you looking to own the franchise for 1 term of 10-years?

- Are you hoping to renew for an additional term?

- Do you want a business that you can sell for a profit within 6 or 7 years?

Any of these questions can give you an idea of what you want your protected territory to be. If you have done your homework and find that the area you want will be profitable and you are willing to work hard, you may want to negotiate for as large of a territory as you can get which will enable you to expand and not saturate your territory in a matter of months or years.

This is an area that is worth thinking about when determining your future with the business. Effectively negotiating for a larger territory will allow your franchised business to expand, thereby reaching more customers, while saving money in the long run by preventing you from having to later purchase a surrounding territory for an additional expense.

Negotiate The Term of Your Franchise

Another effective area to negotiate that can save you money is the term of your franchise. By term, we mean the number of years that you contract with the franchisor to operate the franchised business. Most franchise agreements have a term of 10 years, however some can be as low as 5 years or as high as 20 years. No matter how many years your franchise agreement is for, most franchise agreements only allow for one renewal. The term of the franchise agreement and the renewal are two areas very often left alone in negotiations.

Many good things and a fair amount of money can be saved by negotiating for a longer term with fewer restrictions on renewals. By extending your initial franchise term, it allows you to see a greater return on your investment in the franchise.

Most franchisees will spend their first year or two recovering their initial investment in the franchised business, so negotiating for a 15-year term instead of a 10-year term allows you to spend 5 more years recovering your investment and earning a profit. This extension of time also gives you the opportunity to spend more time looking for a potential buyer that is favorable to the franchisor as well as you, if this is your chosen method out of the franchise system.

Failure to negotiate renewals can spell disaster in some instances when your renewal time approaches. Most franchisees fail to negotiate the renewal terms at the time they negotiate the initial term.

In most franchise systems, there are stringent requirements to renew your franchise including payment of a renewal fee, which can be as high as 50% of the initial franchise fee, renovation of the franchised business, and most importantly the requirement that you must sign the "then current franchise agreement."

By signing the "then current franchise agreement" you may be opening yourself up to higher royalties, advertising fees, and a plethora of other higher fees that you had not incurred previously.

By reviewing these items with your franchisor and franchise attorney prior to signing the franchise agreement, you can potentially save profits for your business instead of your franchisors business in the future.

If you could permanently avoid late fees and pay less in royalties, would you want to? The answer to these questions should be an emphatic yes. However, franchisors continually bait franchisees into paying minimum royalties and tack on late fees when both can be avoided.

When you are late with a fee, either for royalties, advertising, product purchases, etc., you expect a late fee of some sort. However, you should attempt to negotiate with the franchisor to utilize an automatic withdrawal from your business account.

Although this will not prevent you from incurring late fees or overdraft fees if your bank account is too low, it can help to prevent checks for thousands of dollars being lost in the mail, which can save you valuable profits in the end.

Minimum royalties are another way that franchisors can stick you with a bill that depletes your profits unnecessarily. Some franchisors require that you pay a minimum dollar amount in royalties if you do not meet a certain amount of gross sales. These figures can range typically from $100 to $500.

Although this number may not seem like much when, in good months, you may be paying thousands of dollars in royalties, but in slow months, like many franchisees may have seen in recent years, this number can add up quickly if you are not making the gross sales to counteract this minimum royalty payment.

Negotiating for removal of minimum royalties and electing automatic withdrawals are two methods of saving valuable profits that can be reinvested in your franchised business.

Negotiate Non-Competition Agreement

One major aspect to a franchise agreement and one that you may have a hard time getting the franchisor to negotiate on is the non-competition agreement: the non-competition agreement is a contract between you and the franchisor limiting you from managing, owning, and working in a competing business like the franchised business you owned through the franchise system.

A franchisor invests time, effort and money into training you and teaching you the ins and outs of their system and their industry. It is only practical that they want to keep their trade secrets from the rest of the world, especially competitors.

Many non-competition agreements require that you not work in the same industry within a certain number of miles from your previous franchised business, typically 25 – 50 miles, and in some cases from any of the franchised businesses for a certain number of years.

Depending on the state that you are residing in, the strength of the franchisors non-competition contract may be limited; however, it is wise to request that the agreement be negotiated for as short a time period and distance as possible, just in case you chose not to renew with this particular franchisor.

In conclusion

It is always best to have an experienced franchise attorney assist you when negotiating and preparing to negotiate a franchise purchase. Remember, the franchisor has spent tens of thousands of dollars with their attorneys to draft the franchise documents in their favor, not yours.

However, by reviewing some of your strong skills and exploiting some of the franchisors weaker or non-essential points, you may negotiate for your ideal franchise purchase.

In the few instances that a franchisor is steadfast and refuses to negotiate on any section of the franchise agreement, it may be time to reevaluate your choice in franchisors and move on.

For more assistance in these areas, you can read articles published through the International Franchise Association, multiple franchise attorneys' websites, the American Bar Association, and through the Federal Trade Commission.

Your **Notes:**

ABOUT THE AUTHOR AND COMPANY

Asset Exchange Strategies, LLC and Asset Exchange Group, LLC are Owner Managed IRA Advisors; they are not custodians.

Daniel Cordoba is principal and founder of the Asset Exchange Companies. Daniel is a featured regular speaker on Talk Radio shows as well as other financial media such as ABC World news, Wall Street Journal, Forbes, Kiplinger, Realty Times, Business Week and many other major media.

He is the author of "Tax Favorable Real Estate Transactions", a course book approved by the Texas Real Estate Commission, books "From Wall Street To Main Street" focusing on buying specific with your IRA, and "Self-Study Guide on Owner Managed IRA Investing".

Online Bio - Press/Media Site: www.danielcordoba.com

Asset Exchange Strategies and
Asset Exchange Group   www.assetexchangestrategies.com

About Purchasing Real estate

www.myrealestateira.com

Purchase Self Education
Manuals/Guides   www.iratraining.com

Daniel Cordoba

THE KNOWLEDGE LEADER ON ASSET EXCHANGE STRATEGIES

Available For:
Speaking Engagements
Seminar Programs
Personal Consultations
Executive Retirement Planning

Speaker Topics
Exercise Tax Favorable Strategies
Owner Managed Retirement Planning
Leverage Asset & Entity Advantages

Designations
B.A. in Business Management,
University of Phoenix

Professional Licenses
Texas Department of Insurance Life and
Accident Insurance, Texas Real Estate
Commission Instructor, Real Estate
Finance and Real Estate Investments,
NASD Investor Education on
Professional Designations

Contact Information
www.danielcordoba.com
info@danielcordoba.com
866-683-5228

Recognized Leader in education offerings for Owner Managed IRA Investing; Founder and President of Asset Exchange Strategies, LLC; Founder of NATFI, National Association of Tax Favorable Investing

In Detail – Daniel Cordoba is recognized as the expert in asset exchange strategies including Owner Managed retirement investing. He is quoted and featured in numerous high-end media, and continues to be sought out for speaking engagements, advice, and consulting services. He is the Author of the Texas Real Estate Commission approved real estate course: Tax Favorable Real Estate Transactions.

How He Presents – Daniel is a frequent speaker at national investor groups; an instructor to high producing real estate agents, investment talk radio shows, and television news broadcasts. His powerful presentations are packed with a rich source of actionable information, which he expresses with clarity and precision.

Media - Daniel is quoted in Kiplinger's Magazine, Wall Street Journal, Forbes, On Wall Street, Women's Wall Street, Reality Times, CPA journals and other notable online and print media.

ABOUT SHELTON & POWER, LLC

Shelton & Power, LLC, Franchise Attorneys was specifically started to help proven entrepreneurs "Expand their Brand" through a cost effective process of franchise establishment, legal compliance and sales and marketing best practices. With this Mission, the Shelton & Power, Franchise Law Offices were forged. Our pledge is to always give you 100% of our dedication, with flat and discounted legal fees for almost all matters. Our relaxed atmosphere shows you we are just plain folks working hard at what we love.

As a Shelton & Power client, you will receive:

- Welcome Kit which contains a personalized Franchisee Questionnaire

- General problem solving via phone or email from our friendly and professional staff

- The exclusive "Mistakes to Avoid" Publication

- Best Practices Newsletter from Industry Leaders

- Continuing educational insights from the Annual and International Franchise Conventions

We encourage franchisees to seek sound franchise legal advice prior to committing to any franchise system. It is towards that end that we offer blatantly and openly within this book the huge discount on our FDD review services. If you contact us and provide us the coupon code of "Wall Street to Main Street," we will provide your full FDD and Franchise Agreement Review for a flat fee of $1,000.00.

You will receive the same services that other clients pay over twice as much for. We can also offer you discounted rates to guide you with our years of experience in the industry and legal planning. Contact us directly for details.

Lynne Shelton, Esq.
Direct line: 512-968-9922
Office line: 512-535-0090
Facsimile: 512-535-0084

E-Mail: Lynne@SheltonPower.com
Blog: sheltonpower.blog.com
Twitter: FranchiseTweet
LinkedIn: linkedin.com/in/LynneShelton

Lynne has assisted businesses with their franchise and business opportunities since 1993. She especially enjoys working with small business owners to assist them in "Expanding their Brand". As a past franchisor herself, Ms. Shelton understands the needs and growth pains of her clients. While Ms. Shelton has represented both Franchisor as well as Prospective Franchisee, her specialty is in the area of providing experienced counsel for Startup and Emerging Franchisor's who wish to establish or grow into a Regional or National Franchise System.

Her area of expertise transverses many different industries including restaurants, financial systems, construction, interior design, fitness, mining, senior care, and service industries including painting, installation, heating and air-conditioning.

Jason W. Power, Esq.
Direct line: 813-625-9590
Facsimile: 214-594-6533
E-Mail: Jason@SheltonPower.com
Blog: http://sheltonpower.blog.com
Twitter: FranchiseTweet
Linkedin: Linkedin.com/in/JasonPower

Jason Power has been in the legal industry for over 10 years as both a legal assistant and attorney. After spending time in everything from personal injury to property law, Jason found his passion in the franchise law arena.

He works with franchisors to "Expand their Brand" into both foreign and domestic markets; as well helping franchisees evaluate and negotiate a franchise. Handling issues ranging from franchise creation and franchise evaluation to franchise termination, Jason strives to not only represent his clients but also help educate them at the same time.

Muse To Creative Minds

Assisting Change & Growth and Develop

Contact Information
Email: Sonia@accelerprocess.com
Phone: 512.535.3148

Author
The Handbook on Kicking The Aging Habit™, and
Soon to be published: Preparing For & Surviving Joint Replacement

Co-Author

Partnering With Your IRA, and

How To Determine The Self-Directed IRA LLC or 401(k) Plan That Meets Your Needs

Web Sites
www.iratraining.com
www.decideonrealestate.com
www.accelerprocess.com

Social Media
Linkedin Twitter Plaxo
Facebook Google

Strategist, Author, Mentor, Entrepreneur, Health/Fitness Advocate with highly honed collaborative and creative skills.

St. James has extensive business development experience including 25 years as a creative consultant, and over 10 years assisting entrepreneurs to grow and develop products and services.
She is referred to as a Muse.

Founder of the AccelerProcess™
A unique method to assess, clarify and organize your idea, challenge or project; position it's outcome; and develop an action plan to reach your desired goal.

Visit AccelerProcess.com

ISBN 978-0-557-77346-6

9 780557 773466

www.ingramcontent.com/pod-product-compliance
Lightning Source LLC
Chambersburg PA
CBHW081200180526
45170CB00006B/2169